The Presidency of HILLARY CLINTON

ISBN 978-1543015355

Made in the USA
Monee, IL
18 December 2019

19001449R00066